FRAGMENTS

of my Life through

Poetry

Amira Montaque-Bey

Harmony Network
New Jersey

HARMONY NETWORK PUBLISHING
New Jersey

Fragments of My Life through Poetry

ISBN: 978-0-9893483-2-4

Copyright © 2013 by Amira Montaque-BEY

ಐ

Order Fragments of My Life Through Poetry
www.amira123.com

ಐ

Harmony Network www.harmonyllc.org

Edited and Designed by Tea M. Harmony

Printed in the United States of America

This book is dedicated to my baby girl Destini and Tea Harmony. Tea came into my life at a time when I had a great need. Tea I appreciate you.

ACKNOWLEDGEMENTS

GOD
ಬ

God thank you for blessing my children and I. You brought us from a life of destruction to redemption. Thank you for sending your angels to protect us

TEA M. HARMONY
ಬ

Special thanks to Tea for blessing me with your uplifting presence. You are a gift from God. Thank you for making this book a reality. You coached me through the process. You took my notebook and turned it into a book. Being the person that you are inspired me to be the best me. You taught me never to give up! I love you so much!!!

DESTINI
ಬ

Thank you for being strong when we were at a low point. You encouraged me to keep writing; to pick up my pen and pad. I stopped writing when I was 15 because everything positive in me died. You encouraged me to keep writing while we were in the shelter. Thank God for blessing me with a beautiful, smart, funny and down to earth daughter. I love you princess.

MY CHILDREN
ಬ

Daisy: smart and beautiful! You said you want to be a doctor. I believe in you because you believe in yourself. Dreams do come true. Allen a.k.a Papi-I thank God for you. When you fell at two months you could have lost your life but you are here. I thank God for my new son Isaiah....I will always love you, Mommy

DADDY
ဆ

My daddy Governor Abdullah Muhammad-Bey I know
you are shining upon me. May your soul rest in peace. I
Love You.

MS. KAREN
ဆ

I love your uplifting spirit. You are a beautiful
sistah to be around. The way you speak your poetry
is just wonderful! I love you always.

TULINA
ဆ

From the moment we met, we clicked. You are my
sister that I never had. We started talking like we
knew each other for years. I love you and I wish
you and your family nothing but the best.

TAWANA
ဆ

Thank you for being there for me at 'Glam Day'.
You and your family are always in my heart.

CONTENTS

CONTENTS

CONTENTS

ళ

Chapter VII – Family

Chapter VIII- Helping Hands

Chapter IX – God's Blessings

Chapter X – Inspiration

CONTENTS

ಶಿ

Chapter XI – The Breakthrough

**Chapter XII –
God's Money vs. The Devil's Money**

Chapter XIII – Obstacles

CONTENTS

ဆ
Chapter XIV– Learning

Chapter XV
Life is Much Better Now

Fragments

of My *Life* through

Poetry

Lexington Terrace
Chapter I

Lexington Terrace

I was born and raised in the 770 building
Where nigga's were shot and killed
Where drugs flowed for real
My mother tried to cover my eyes
I saw dead bodies surrounded by flies

My mother despised the situation
The traffic and the jealous nigga's hating
Grandma wanted to stay
Always had tricks up her sleeve
She just did not want to leave

She loved the limelight
Drinking Cat Eye's and Colt 45
She loved that building for seventeen years
Even though her own son was shot down and killed

Then she realized it was time to go
The show she put on had to end

Friend after friend
She could not trust

While the son she loved
Now six feet under in the dust

Miracle Baby

Laying in the hospital
On my death bed
The doctor said I'm dead

The pastor, the family
Maybe God is giving me a second chance
I'm Praying, wishing and hoping I don't leave this
earth
In my heart, it's just a rebirth

What I haven't endured
Now I have seen the light
It's time to explore

Time to do what I have to do
In the process of giving it all back to you

Booker Cherry

My Uncle
Booker
He was a good man
Shot in the head
Damn, now he's lying there dead

Bleeding
Laying on the ground
At the Reptile House
Druid Hill Park
All playing out after dark

Shoes on his feet
Couldn't dodge the heat of that gun
He thought this life of selling drugs was fun

His mother knew
Knew his life would end
She just didn't know when
The life of her son would end
at the hands of his so-called friend

Only 5

Dec 7, 1984
Death came knocking at my door
I saw the light
Then God said, you don't have to worry anymore
You are a blessing
Forevermore

In a coma
Didn't know how to walk
Had to learn all over again
God had me
He is my friend

A praying mother
Way back when
She made a wish back then

That God would Bless Me
And my life would not have to end

Grandmother Raised Me

I was too young to see
Didn't understand why this had to be
My mother didn't raise me
Then she had my brother Rasheed

Yea, I had asthma
Grandma said she smoked a lot of weed
She was my guide
The one I looked up to
Didn't know why life was so mean

I use to lay in bed
With the covers over my head
Wanting this nightmare to be over

Seven years later
My mother said she understand
Now that I am much older

Family Curse
Chapter II

FAMILY CURSE

Mother, Father
Sister, Brother, Grandmother
Step Grandfather, Aunts and Uncles
In this cold house

Started from the roots of broken vessels

Everybody is Mad
Without reason
Different Generations
Seasons of ....

Hatred
Lies
Sex
Molestation

And the penetration of everything evil...
I am determined to stop this curse
Decided to put my God first
My Seeds will grow

In Love....In Peace....In Happiness
and it all will show, I'm breaking the Family Curse

House but Not a Home

Here in this big house
All Alone
No one to call my Own

Blue
Black
Dark colors is all I've seen
On the flip side
This house is always clean

Made people wonder you know
How all these pretty things were just for show

Here in this big house
All Alone
No one to call my Own

This House is not a Home

NAME CALLING

Bitch, Slut, Stupid, Crazy

Ugly ass, Spineless ass Man

Never liked him
but the Money was always in his hand

Baldheaded

Dummy

Ignorant Fool

No education
He dropped out of school

She worked at the hospital
He worked for the city
Although he treated her shitty
She knew she was pretty

Pretty on the outside
Broken within
She could never let go
She never had God, You Know

Names is what he called her
That's what she answered to
This is what a girl like me lived through

MATERIAL THINGS

Jewelry
Watches
Gold Rings

Nice furniture and Pretty Things
Money, Cars and Expensive Things

All this
All that
But where is the love at?

There's no Love
How could this be?
It's the light not the darkness
That comes with Eternity

Material things can't buy love or happiness
These Material things
Can never replace the freedom and joy that Jesus
brings

NOBODY'S THERE

I felt like a bear without its' fur
All this evil had to occur
Sitting back in the corner
Did not know it scorned her

Physically
Emotionally
FOR LIFE

ONLY ME

Nobody's There
Far, Far apart
Just ME

Trapped in this world
A Lost Little Girl
With Nobody there

MOMMY & DADDY

The both of y'all had me
A Beautiful Baby Girl
Pretty Brown Skin
Head full of curls

Mommy and Daddy
Loved me
But left me in this world

Mommy and Daddy left their Beautiful Baby Girl

To fend for myself "Really!"

My tender eyes saw a lot
Things that left mental scars
That was my reality

My Mommy and My Daddy
Donated the Egg and the Sperm
Thank You for it all
Because I had to Learn

Rebellion

Chapter III

REBELLION

You can't tell ME what to do
I am resisting you
Not listening to what you have to say
What the Hell!
Nobody cares anyway

Always Yelling
Cannot express what's on your mind
So why do I have to come in the house
At this time

Not listening
I don't care what you say
Listen! I will NOT
Let me find MY Own Way!

AGE 11

Do Good
Go to Heaven
Period

If I do Good
I'll go to Heaven

I learned at an early age
Felt like a prisoner locked in a cage

House of Horror
No one to Bother
I just wanted my Mother and Father

Everybody doing their Own Thang
So I hit the streets
I wanted to hang

Anger at Eleven
All that I knew
My heart is hurting
What is a girl Like ME to do?

A Friend

I was Eleven
She was only Nine
Young girls exploring
Damn she was fine

I did the things I've seen
Her mother was a crack fein
She loved me
Although my family was mean

That was my friend

Scramble eggs and pancake mix
She taught me how to cook
All while her mother looked for her next fix

Life was like a bad storm
But we managed to keep each other warm

She was my Friend

MIRROR, MIRA

Mirror, Mira on the wall
My name means Princess
The best of them all

Looking into the glass that hung on the wall
Was not prepared for the hard fall

Why?
How could this be?
There's nobody here to ride with me

Mirror, Mira
I thought nobody cared
Left alone
To fight my fears

Mirror, Mira

You can't see my tears

MY EYES

These Eyes of Mine saw so much
Both positive
      And negative
Yet I'm still in touch

From the start
I knew kindness
I knew how to give from my heart

Sexual abuse
These Eyes of Mine have seen
I saw my step Grandfather and Aunt
And Granny never said a thing

A little girl's Eyes
These eyes are trapped
by my fears and tears

Wishing I could erase the pain
      of this sick life
I've seen in vain

A lot of fears, My Tears couldn't erase the pain
Of all the sickness
I've seen
These eyes of mine are clean

OUTSIDE

Fresh air
Green trees
The atmosphere
At its best
It helped me escape from all this mess

Escaping my thoughts
Of people, places and things
People not living right
Just plain ole mean

Kids always want to ride
Taking turns on my bike
Auntie loved her some women
She was proud to be a dyke

The fresh air
Helped me cope
The aroma changed my mood
I felt better about life

Outside was my shelter
Better than that empty, cold, cold house
Where nobody cared
Where the little girl in me lived
Scared

Outside was my air
The trees my companion
A different view, you see
Knowing I could handle

The truth of my reality

Confidence it gave me
Little girl on my own
Being outside
With the air and the trees
I was never all alone

Good Girl
Gone Bad

Chapter IV

Good Girl Gone Bad

It's all good
I thought
Hanging with the boys in the hood
Exposed too soon
Experiences I've seen
Testing the surface
Doing the wrong things

Look at Me
As I stare, in my mirror
I don't care
Ready to fight
Whoever steps in my life

Fuck the world
And the people in it

It was all good
So I thought
That hood shit is so sad
Sometimes it will make a Good Girl
Go Bad

My First Love

A Superstar
So I thought

Good looks
I was off the hook

He did it for me
At 15 I gave myself to him
    Sexually

Felt like he would be the death of me

In love with this guy
He was so fly

As I lay in his arms
He was my charm

Like chocolate melting away
My first love
Made me feel this way

Hustling Type Nigga's

Bad boys is what I admired
Pulling them triggers
Yeah go figure

Real bad nigga's
Mug shot taking nigga's
Drug selling type nigga's
Hip hop listening type nigga's

Making money nigga's
Shopping at the mall
They had all the cuties
Me
One of them all

Honey's on the hip
I thought it was slick
Even jail on the agenda
He was sexing me and Brenda

I didn't care what that life was about
Hustling nigga's who get down without a doubt

Caught Up

Sitting around looking stupid and stuck
Was it only me?
His grandmother tried to warn me
But a sista like me
Didn't want to hear nothing

That's why he dissed me

He's the center of my attraction
My heart is the center of hurt
My emotions left me stuck in the dirt

I'm Caught Up

I'm all caught up
I lost myself
Not concerned or worried about my health

I'm Caught Up

Here I go again
Caught up to the point where I cut my leg
Left again holding the bag
Caught Up over a guy
That I never had

Heartbreak

That's what they do
Whisper lies in your ear
Tell you what you want to hear

His words became my God
All for His purpose
Always
Only
To awaken my love

Deceived by the mystique of his language
Lustful lies seemingly true
If I wasn't so caught up
But then again, I knew

Youthful lust
Claiming to love
Heartbreak it caused

That's what he did to me
This heartbreak
Was a catastrophe!

LOOKING FOR LOVE

....in ALL the Wrong Places

Chapter V

Looking for Love....
In All the Wrong Places

Different faces
Guys and Girls
Sexing and lusting
In this crazy world

But is it crazy?
The world that is
Or do we choose our path
by the way we live

Thought it was ok
For a guy and a girl
To be sexing and lusting this way

Looking for Love
Lust found me
All in my inner spaces
While I was
Looking for Love in All the wrong places

17 and 33

I was still a teenager
but in his mind he said I could raise her!

16 years older than me
I was looking for love
I thought he was my dynasty!!

I did not know any better
I thought he would be there
Despite any type of weather

17 and 33

Just a little girl lost
Trying to be loved you see

S.T.D.

On the wake up
O' Morning rise
Pussy not feeling right

Milky, White discharge
It was then I knew
His Dick was in charge

Doctors' say
It's an S.T.D.
Thoughts flowing
Through my head

Wondering what could it be?

Now I'm really sad
Worried
Thinking of what's wrong with me

O' Morning rise up
Sista got a sick Pussy

Lost
Don't know what to do
This brother, as usual
Don't have a clue
He don't care what I'm going through

Sick Pussy
Oh, this ain't Cute!
A dose of real truth

All I wanted was love
Yea, and sex too

More than what I desired
Yes, Pretty ole me
This Brother
Generously gave me an S.T.D.

PREGNANT!

Now I'm 18
And I'm having his baby
Never thought I wasn't his lady

The man of my dreams
At least it seemed
Left, with a baby
A baby with real needs
     A baby I can't afford to feed

Now I'm 18
18, Pregnant and all alone
Guess I was his lady
     until the day I conceived his baby

ON MY OWN

I thought he would come home
My first apartment
He left us all alone
Just me and my baby
The two of us holding it down

I'm feeling crazy
Thought I was grown
Now I'm sitting here on my own

I put him first
Like My King on His throne
Now silly me
Sitting here, left all alone

But it was good that I'm on my own
When that spirit came around
He only brought wrath

Now I have peace and joy
And sometimes I even laugh....

Fighting for What's Mine

Wilding out
Possessive and all
Waiting for a chick to make that call

I'd smack a chick
Quick
Nobody could be in his face
I was ready to dismiss and erase
Jealousy got so bad
I even caught a case

Fighting for What's Mine
So I thought!
Then I woke up and realized
It was his fault!

Grateful for this experience
A Lesson well taught

<u>Love is Not Suppose to Hurt!</u>

Dag
I really wanted our relationship to work
Did not realize you were a jerk

Clouded by images of falsehood polarized by my
emotion
Being faithful
Holding strong to my devotion

Threatened
Victimized
You telling me what to do
If I refused
My eye would be black and blue

Love is not suppose to hurt
It's suppose to help
Lift up
And make you better

Now I'm hurt, abused and fed up!

The Break Down

Blinded
And I could not see
Mentally, sexually and emotionally
He was breaking me down
Piece by piece

Not sure how much more I could take
Praying that heaven would open up
        For my sake

Not this face
Fashioned and formed by God
By design
Not for his hands to hit
But to touch maybe even caress
        Can't take it anymore

Too much stress
I'm breaking down
Don't want to face tomorrow
Overpowered by the stronghold
        Of my sorrow

Drugs, Sex and Money

Chapter VI

Drugs, Sex and Money!

This world
A life of sex, drugs and money
Life is funny
Sad turned inside out

This world
Full of cheating nigga's
Living two or three lives
Caught up in their own world
Chasing not only women
But lusting after little girls

Sexuality in limbo
At a crossroad
Influenced by the social mold
Nature vs. culture
That's what we're told

Lust----Deceit----Lies----Mystique

Who's straight?
Who's looking for bait?

Baited and hooked
Can't cope
Trying to fill the need
Through pills, liquor and weed

The love of money is no good
But take heed
Money is money when you have a habit to feed

Embracing Experiences
Learning Lessons
Cherishing Failures

Surviving----Life----Drugs----Sex and money
Sometimes ain't a damn thang funny

<u>Being a Dancer</u>....

All that action!
Night lights
Booze
Music
High heel shoes

Me...
Dancing
Mirror, Mira

The center of attraction
Dancing
Prancing
Lovin' it
Shakin' it

Shake
Twirl
Shake
Bounce

Mirrors
Sweat
Smoke
Red lights

Poles
Hoes
Barely clothed

Money
Money
Everywhere
Ready to drop my underwear

No care in the world
Amused and feeling myself
Never thought I would hurt someone else

Madam

Madam
That's what they called me
I said it
They did it
We made it pop
        Got that money!

Big pimping
Lady cartel
Monopolizing their submission
        Using my position

Taking mine off the top
Go get em girls
Take off them tops

You know what they want
Give em a good show
Be a good hoe

Bring my money
So I can eat
So we can eat
After I break you off a piece

Shout out to my hunnies
        Saluting Madam with that money!

Shuga Daddies

Shuga Daddies
Promises
Lies
All to a little girls demise

Calling him daddy
So out of place
Shuga Daddy

Money
Sex and gifts
Drinking and smoking spliffs

They promise to make you
Only to break you
Bind you
While they grind on you

Your body
Your mind
Your soul

This lusting society
Disgust and discourage me
From being the princess
          God created in me

Family

Chapter VII

Family

Deceit
Lies
Binds
Ties

That's the family that I know

That's my family
Not each other's keeper
Selfish
Sneaky

Ready to attack
In this family
You better watch your back

That's the family that I know

It's a Shame
Who will claim?
The blame
Of this family
Deep in pain
Or is it all in vain?

That's the family that I know

Five Years Later

Another baby
Tolerating
All this hating

Dealing with deception
In the midst of intercepting
        His punch to my face
This shit got to end
That's when the empathy began….

5 Years Later
He was my lover
Sex partner at best
A friend
        I thought
Ladies, you know the rest
Thought I was blessed
        Failed this test
Made a damn mess
Got this pain in my chess

Two babies
Second time around
Maybe this time he'll beat me to the ground

5 years later
In this same place
Looking at the Mira

The Mira of disgrace
The Mirror in my face

Destini's Eyes

Mommy & Daddy
Fussing & Fighting

Baby girl, trapped in this melee
No one listening, to what she had to say

Mommy & Daddy
Fussing & fighting
Day and night
This was our life

Seen through the Eyes of Destini

As she grew, She knew
Daddy was mean
With her eyes, She has seen

Seen a lot growing up

Mommy hit daddy
Daddy beat mommy
God intervened

He saw Destinis' eyes
Mommy and Daddy split
Not to her demise

Having both parents is a dream come true
Yet it's not God's plan
To have her father as my man!!

2 Days before Christmas

Niggas just don't care
They just don't know
What it feels like to be thrown out in the cold

Ole dude, put me and His kids out!
Out in the snow
This is a heavy load

Didn't have a plan
No where to go

He's caught up in the evil of this world
2 days before Christmas
He forgot about his two little girls

God Knows My Need!

Inspite of my faults and unnecessary deeds
God looks out for fools and babies

Without understanding
Things still happen

I won't question God
I'll learn to trust in God

I know he has good plans in store
I will keep the faith
Persevere and Endure

God Knows My Need!

Helping Hands
Chapter VIII

Helping Hands

A helping hand
What a beautiful gift
Those hands that won't push you down
Those hands that lift

What a blessing
A helping hand can bring
Through the pressures and injustices
Helping hands can safeguard your dreams

Through the seasons
For more than one reason
They guide
Not divide
They direct
They protect

With their heart
They raise
and through this journey
God gets all the praise

God uses people to do his work
God will always send us helping hands

Mother

We only get one
There's no one like you
You stayed by my side
Although I made you blue

Wrong choices
Disrespectful ways
Disappointment
And tears filled your days

Confusion sought to keep you dazed
Yet your strength stood forth
I am still amazed

We only get one
There's no one like you
You were there
When times were good
When time turned blue

Tough love you gave
Your wild child you sought to save
Glad I had time to write this
Before we entered the grave

Forgive me
I forgave you
I let go of my anger and fears
Surrendered it all to God
Your daughter,
I had to shift gears

We only get one
One mother in this life time
I appreciate your sacrifices
Your My Queen
My lifeline...

From Mira

Jealousy

Jealousy….

You hate me
Because you hate you

Jealousy
Human nature's deadly disease
Hidden
Disguised
As love inside out

Sneaking
Plotting
Deceiving all along

Thought we were friends
I knew I didn't belong

I'll pray for you
That you will get over it
Before that disease Jealousy
Permanently keep you sick

I Forgive You

I surrender
I surrender it all
I'm letting go of the past

Thoughts, memories and experiences
I cast
Mere unforgiveness will not last

I'm seeking
Praying
Asking God to soften my heart
Cleanse me
Wash me
Give me a New start

I Forgive You!
I set you free
From the burden of your sin
Live your life
My friend

This after life
I'm sure will be fun
God will be pleased
That's why He gave his only begotten son

I send you
Peace
Love and happiness

Through forgiveness

There's no more sadness
But mere gladness

I had to forgive you
That's the right thing to do
The forgiveness is for me but it will benefit
You

God's Blessings
Chapter IX

God's Blessings

Stressing and stressing
Letting things get the best of me
Ignorant, not knowing
It's a part of my destiny

Daily when I get up to start my day
I'm overwhelmed
Blessed
Knowing that he woke me up today

I didn't know God allows things to happen
To strengthen our faith
Through hardship and pain
I've learned
That's the case

He did his part
That day on the cross
He died for our sins
It's up to us if we win

Yet we cannot win all on our own
We shall look to God sitting on His throne

His blessings storm down like spring rain
As his love wipes away my pain

God's blessings
Lead me beside still water
Restoring and renewing his precious daughter

God Inside of Me

It's the God in me
At first I was blind
I could not see

Had to dig deep
Deep down inside of me
To acknowledge that abuse
Is the misuse of me

Abuse is an issue
Tussle after tussle
Fist upon fist
Tissue after tissue

Could not stop my tears
I began to see my fears

I said to myself
Mira, just let him go
Let that man be
One day he will see the God inside of me

Change comes from you
Beating after beating
I got tired of being black and blue

Now it's time for me to shine
I'm waiting for God's perfect time

God, my father
Gave me the key
He let me see
That there's a God inside of Me!

The Bus Ride

It's time to get on board
Starting over, Moving on
Time to board this bus

My children and I
Are riding high
Looking forward

To a new life
Free from bondage, pain and strife
On this bus ride
Where miracles begin
Relocating to New York
We're going to win

Not sure what to expect
In this big ole city
We learned real quick
That some people can be shitty

If I could turn back
I would not
My precious gift is time
Now I'm settled
Ready to unwind

All praises to God
It was a phase
Right where I needed to be
God was always guiding me
Even to New York City
At the right time he opened my eyes
That I may see

The Bus Ride!

Domestic Violence Shelter

Reflecting on my life
More than enough time to sit
Thinking of my choices
And all that's passed my way

Though I'm angry
Though I'm tired
My faith is here
I'm looking toward a new day

A better attitude
Shaking off the shackles
Shackles of being rude

A new me
For the world to see
A new lady
Representing my precious babies

This shelter
Here I stand
Looking toward brighter days

Reflecting on my blessings
More than enough time to think
Grateful for life

Thanking God for his refuge and protection
In this domestic violence shelter

Every Day Struggle

Every day it's a struggle

Fighting
Trying
To focus
Some may not notice
Now I depend on this substance

Trying to maintain
Trying to hold it together
Life is making me insane
These drugs messing with my brain

Nursing my habit
Daily I do the same thing
My soul is bound
I Must get clean

This struggle got me shackled
The drugs got the power
Fighting for freedom
Losing by the hour

This fight is like the wind
Hard to bend; hard to grasp
Today, I'll try something new
Allow it to pass
Cause today may be my last

Don't Look Back

Remembering the beatings
15 years of abuse
Though it was out of order
Staying was of no use

Drama became the norm
Night after night
Storm after storm

Shock
Depression
Life changing trauma
This is when a girl really needs her mama

Don't look back
I told myself
Get yourself together
Remain in good health

Use each experience
To help you survive
Move forward
Change your thinking as you strive

I will not look back
I'm staying on track
Looking ahead
To wonderful things
Instead

The memories are an ally to me

A point of reference
And sometimes peace
Not to choose that life again

Although I'm not going back
Although I will not look back
I cherish my life
I embrace my experiences
For they have become my friend

FREE

I am Free
I am Me

I never thought this day would be
I left the man I once loved the most

I am Free, I am Me

Love desires to give
Not take my dignity away
After the sex
I felt dirty and led astray

Yet here I stand
Stronger
Bolder

After those beatings
My heart grew colder
Though I am blessed
I took too much mess

No longer his whore
Lust is out the door

Shaking the dust of my feet
Because I am Free
I am Me
I am becoming the person
I never thought I could be

I'm Sweet, Pleasant, Kind
Now I can rest
Rest with a peace of mind

Inspiration
Chapter X

Inspiration

Inspired

Flying high
A natural high

Blessed

Tonight was a beautiful night
The night I met Tea

She spoke to me
She taught me
That I can become all that I could be
I am the possibility
No matter what my situation suggest

Right now I'm in this DV Shelter
My life is a hot mess
But God uses people
Black women with power

To inspire and empower

I was honored to be in their presence
These women treated me kind
Then I knew
I felt God

I left Baltimore for a reason
To meet these women
Even for just a season

They told me they'd be there
Their spirits showed that they care

Tea, do your best and pray I won't settle for less
These words are not just a note
I send you love, peace and hope

I am blessed and inspired
No longer will I get tired
I'm keeping my faith
Giving God the rest
Thriving to pass this test

A Lesson Well Taught

Life will take you places
People will teach you things

Experiences I cherish
Patterns and levels I'm living

I fought to get here
A hard journey to live
My lessons taught me that they really didn't care

Family and fake friends
Did not want to see me prosper

If it was up to them
I would amount to nothing
But God
Saw fit that his daughter turn into something

Beautiful
Smart
Black sister

Glad God didn't overlook
And miss her

I'm letting people go
Saying my goodbye's
I will live this life
Praising God
I will lift my hands to the sky
Thank God for a lesson Well Taught

Adapting

Adapting can be hard
But you must open your heart
To receive
Receive everything new

A new situation
I'm taking it all in

Different atmosphere
Different nationalities
A lot of changes
This is my reality

Buses
Trains
Long walks
These eyes of mine
They see

Kids playing in the park
Loud music
Candles lit in the dark

The food
The water
Everything is different
Than where I come from

Adapting can be hard
But you must open your heart
To receive
Receive everything new

Adapting is different
By adapting I've been uplifted

TULINA

Your words have changed my life
It helped me work through the pain and the strife

Your words are better than milk and honey
It's more valuable than any amount of money

Your ears are always open
Your shoulder is always free
Thank you for letting me know
That you are in this with me

There were times we were on the phone
You heard the pain in my voice
Through your compassion and love
I found a way to rejoice

Thank you again, from my heart to your ears
I'm starting over again
I'm blessed with positive years

Tulina, your words have touched me so
I will cherish and remember
I will never let those moments go

A Gift from God

Talents, gifts and abilities
Hidden under my finger tips
Words, poems and letters
Flowing from my lips

Expressing, Interacting, Experiencing

Things that I have seen
These words I speak
Should always be clean

God blessed me!

He gave me insight
Based on everything I went through
I never knew these words would bless others

I was writing for myself
Words of encouragement
Drawing from His well
His well of nourishment

A gift from God
That's what I've been given
God blessed my spirit, kissed my soul
Spoke through me, and made me whole

It's my Gift from God!

The Breakthrough
Chapter XI

The Breakthrough

There's calm
After the storm
It's a breakthrough

Starting over
It's a brand new day
It was all a test
Leading me

So long
To what was
Yesterdays' blues
I'm moving beyond
That's old news

I'm breaking through
Birthing a new part of me
A piece of me
I've never seen

Surrounded by sound wisdom
Got my sword, the bible
My music, for inspiration
This breakthrough
Within my heart sensations

There's calm
After the storm
Be alarmed….
It's my breakthrough
I'm coming strong!

The Devil in Disguise

Beauty displayed
Motives conveyed
Plans to capture me
Thwarting fear

These devils, never sincere

My brown eyes
Caught up in your lies
Disguised
All to my demise
Yeah, I was your prize

These devils
Always near
But beware
They're never sincere

Covering Up

Cover it up
Don't expose your body
My daddy Governor Abdullah Mohammed-Bey
would say

Life is not innocent and simple
Baby girl, your body is your temple

Praying to Allah
Five time a day
Daddy said it was supposed to be this way

Wash your hands, face, ears and feet
Prayer rug, Quran
It's not defeat

It's sacred
Respect it
Pray over it
Clean it

Cover it up
My daddy would say
Life is not innocent and simple
Baby, treat your body like a temple

Demons All Around

Spirits…Floating…Invisible…Intangible

Demons all around me

Evil seeking to capture
Kill, Demolish, Destroy

Demons all around me

Though I can't see them
I know they exist
Spirits floating
Invisible, intangible

They hide and seek
Spirit and soul
This realm is cold
Waiting for events to unfold

Demons all around me

You can't lose
Trust the Voice
….of the Holy Spirit
Be Alert! Pay attention!
Open your heart , Give ear
Know that God is near

Trust Only One

I put myself through it
Got way off track
Just for a short while
Then I bounced back

Trying to figure it out
This thing called life
Learning and growing
Through the pain and strife

Then I learned a lifelong lesson
I count it a blessing
When folks let me down
God's care is always there

He's the only one I can count on
He's the only one I can trust

Gods Money

vs.

The Devils Money

Chapter XII

Gods Money vs. the Devils Money

Everything that glitter is not gold
It's hard to control
When that paper fold
Profit the world
Lose your soul

It's Gods' money vs. the devils' money
Behold! For the love of money is deceptive
Building wealth is accepted
Don't get caught up
Loving the thing that should serve you

When you use it right
It will bless not curse you

It's Gods' way vs. the devils'
You choose!

Open your Bible

Open your bible

Read
Gain understanding
God is coming back
Just as he planned

He is…
Alpha
Omega
It can't get any greater

An abundant life
Affection
Beauty
And protection

Comforter
Deliverer
There's no one greater

Open your bible
Discover his character
The stories of our lives

Knowledge and wisdom belong to you
When you open your bible
You will see what God can do

What God has For Me!

What God has for me
Is for me

My portion is secure
He said it in his word

What God has for me
I BELIEVE!

In a world of
Lust
Lies
And hurt
God is a man of good works

I have the victory
These brown eyes, now see
That what god has for me
Is for me

Still Standing

I am Here!

I declare I am Here!

I'm Still standing

In peace
In wisdom
A part of His kingdom

I am Here!
I declare I am Here!

I'm Still Standing

In Strength
In Submission
In Serenity
I'm finding my identity

In His Love
I'm still standing

Thank you Jesus

Thank you Jesus
For the precious life you gave me

You opened my eyes
You helped me see

Thank you Jesus
For saving a girl like me

I am an overcomer
In a world of pain and misery

It is only because
Your presence lives in me

A Family that Pray Together Stay Together

Every night we kneel to pray
Thanking God for His mercy and grace
For supplying all of our family needs
For His care concerning me

His love keeps shining on us
In so many ways
That's why we bow down
To give him praise

For a family like ours
A Family who pray together
We've weathered the storms
And we stayed together

Angels All Around Us

They go before me
Protecting and speaking to me
I have angels all around me

The spirit can attest
These sensations and feelings
Are real
These angels are on my side
Making an appeal

Guiding us
Providing clear direction
Wrapped in love and affection

I have angels all around me
Oh what an earthly blessing

Obstacles

Chapter XIII

Obstacles

Obstacles
Stacked high
Olympics
Pushing to Win
This race

These obstacles
Keep looking in my face
Abuse showed up
Looking for a place to stay

I told him
Leave
Stay away

Today
I'm the head
No longer the tail
Move
I'm not going to fail

Sleepless nights
Are over
No more fights

I'm standing strong, I'm free

Thank you God for saving me!

Back Again....
A Journey back to B-More

I'm back!
Back in B-more
Been gone for a minute
Thirteen months, Eleven Days
Dealing with the same people
Behaving the same ways

Another baby----Another beginning
Back in B-More
He tried to come back in

A new woman----New experiences----Moving
beyond
Where I used to live

The enemy thinks he got this
Surrounded by the darkness----Setting up traps----
Laughing
Trying to win my soul back

I'm back in B-More
But B-More is not back in me

I say no
No to this B-More Life
I say no to the strife
Feeding this trifling life

I've been some places
Met some people

Changed while I visited the city
No more defeat
No more pity

A new woman
New experiences
Moving beyond
Where I used to live

Back in B-More
But B-More is not in me
I'm a new kind of tree
I'm a new kind of me

Feelings

Healing
Kneeling
Growing
Feeling

My feelings
Learning the difference
Between Love and Lust
My feelings are learning how to trust

I'm moved
I'm led
By the invisible flow
Though not physical form
It's my feelings, yearning to keep you warm

Healing
Yielding
Growing
Feeling

Exploring
Trusting
Discovering

Waiting to find love again

Snakes

Sneaky
Slimy
Gutter
Grimy

Poisonous serpents
Using my weakness as bait
Those venomous snakes

Deceit and Confusion
Darkness and misusing
Trying to bruise me
Those snakes want me to lose

Sneaky
Slimy
Gutter
Grimy
Snakes

I'm following God
Changing my life
I'm determined to win this fight

The Shelter
Balto County

Travelling but Sheltered

Shelter to shelter
Different time
Different place
Back in the County

My children are tired
Another Ninety days
Another state; time to wait
More workers with flaky ways

Travelling but Sheltered

Another shelter
Looking for stability
Warding off the stress in me

Lit up that smoke
Needed to cope
Lost sight
Almost lost hope

People testing and tempting me
But they can't see
God has a plan for me

The Devil is a Liar

Darkness, a presence within the light
The light illuminated the darkness
Shining through its' motives
Prepared to extinguish it

The Devil is a Liar

It is his job
To steal and destroy
To cover up his cunning ways
To lie and bring chaos through our days

Corruption
Interruption
Destruction

Darkness belongs to the devil
To feed and give life to all evil
Darkness tries to kill the light
But the light illuminates through the darkness

I Pray

Father, I pray
This day for your continued help

Bless and protect my children
Forgive me of my sin

Your works are wonderful
Everything you do
I'm grateful that I am here
Just to pray
To you

Lead me to holiness
I know that's your will for me
Open my eyes through your word
Help me to be a better me

Make me whole
Open my soul

Behold, I come
Bold before you
I pray this day
Father continue to make a way

When God is in the Building

When God is the building
He won't steer you wrong
Even if the answers take too long

Disregard what the world may say
God is God
He always makes a way

When God is in the building
He will lead you right
He's there throughout your fight

Give it to him
He wants more of us
Oh, he's glorious!

When God is in the building
He is healing and delivering

He's in the building
Planting seeds
Supplying all of my needs

He is the gospel
In him, know that
All things are possible

Learning
Chapter XIV

Learning

Daily, I learn
Whether positive
Or negative
I'm still learning

When I learned that Jesus' love
Gives, endlessly
When I learned that He never changes
Even when I change

Daily, I learn
My life has changed
When I learn new information
My foundation is solid

I'm still learning

Growing and maturing
A single mother at hand
Raising righteous one's
According to God's plan

Now I can truly see
That Jesus is the best thing
That ever happened to me
When I stumble and when I fall
Jesus' hand holds me through it all

Teach Her

God will send you a guide
Right when you need one
Through my travels He was there
He sent a man to look after me
One who cares

A Teacher

Now I'm back in B-More
Your thoughts and words
Are still in my head
Time and distance cannot separate us

You are still my teacher
Daily I look to your wisdom for clarity
Thank you for teaching me to read and write
Giving me a deeper understanding

Forever
I am grateful that God sent you to me
I'm glowing
I'm growing
I'm learning
Because you planted these seeds

Patience

Be still
Wait on me
Train your head and heart
To embrace the process

Patience is calling to you

Suffering will only last a while
Trust in your father
Cast your cares, my child

Believe
Take action and do nothing
Understanding the times
God's purposes will arrive
On time

Embrace virtue
Not anxiety
Stand strong
You belong
To a world of possibilities
A world of infinite power

God is not done
Patiently wait
The best is yet to come

A Better Understanding

I've learned to let go
That's why
Today
I am better

It did not require
High school or college
God gave me a gift
He gave me knowledge

He changed my heart
He challenged my mind
He gently pushed
At times demanded

He did it for me
To gain a better understanding

Faith and Believe

Faith believes in the invisible
Until it manifest in the physical
Faith is action
It can be achieved
Open your heart to receive

Faith will lead
Help you succeed
Through the highs and the lows
Believe and you will see

God is willing
He's strengthening your belief
Challenging the thief

One who seeks to Kill, Destroy and Steal
What you are trying to build

Have Faith and Believe

Hold On

Just Hold On
When the strings weaken
And the answers slip from your grasp
Hold on and don't let go

Avoid negative people and situations
Seeking to poison you with conversations
Go beyond their limited ways
Walk toward righteousness
For your name sake

Just Hold on
You can take it
Believe in your ability
Understand you can make it

When the strings weaken
And the strands begin to tear
Bend your knees
Raise your hands
Bask in Prayer

Wait on the Lord

He will never leave
Cleave to Him
As you trust

You are cared for
The one who matters the most
Thank and Praise
Our heavenly host

Mind, Body
Soul and Spirit

Listen for His voice
Grab hold, As your hear it

Wait on the Lord

Even when things seem slow
Keep waiting
The promises will soon flow

Your desires is His will
Seek Him first
He's going to fulfill

Be patient
Be still! Relax and Chill
Just wait on the Lord

At Peace

It's been 33 years
Situations
Experiences
Breakdowns
Fears

I'm at Peace.

Rebuilding my heart and mind
Grateful for it all
Capturing the moment
In time

I'm at Peace.

Maintaining
Balancing the demands
A Strong mind, A Sane Soul
Now in control

Reaching
Moving
Going forward
Dodging negative influences
Focused on my destiny

Petty ignorance
Annoying hindrance
Penetrating my innocence
But this peace I have
It's intense
It's a fence coming to my defense
I'm at Peace.

Life is . . .much better now

Chapter **XV**

Life is Much Better Now

I thought no one could hear me
Until I heard my Voice
In between the lies and cussing
Laughing and fussing

I heard
Streams of clarity
Paddling my doorsteps
My heart sprung open
to the melody of triumph

Though Life can be a challenge
God you always manage
To help me take advantage
of each opportunity

Life is much better now

During those times
Our bond became stronger
No trial can break it
Then my heart flutters
Telling me I can make it

Life is much better now

So for starters
I give thanks and praises
Because life would be much harder
Without the help of my dear father

Not Just a House....Our Home

Our Home
A place of comfort
A room of my own

Sheltered, Covered, Provided for
Though not in vain
As I look around
I won't complain

I'll keep praying and thanking God
For my Now
Ignoring the devil
Patiently waiting on my crown

God keeps blessing me
There's no room for
Gravity

From shelter to shelter
Out on my own
But today,
I have my own

Filled with love and laughter
This house is not a house
It's a home

My Children

On that cross
You died for me
So I could see the day
You blessed my seed

My children
Father you gave
A heritage
For me to raise

Thank you Lord
They are precious
Protect and build them up from negativity
Lead them in the way of right living and simplicity

Allow them to lead
And follow when necessary
Thank you for their gifts, talents and abilities
Continue to mold their lives
My children, a gift from God

Look at Me Now

I'm better than before
Now, I have a glow
God's blessings
They overflow

The score is
100
99
and a half won't do

Look at Me Now
No worries or tears
I left the past in the dust
With all of my fears

Experiences they come
As the years go
A new life has begun
As the blessings go up
I'm grabbing each one

Look at Me Now
The woman in the mirror
I left that baggage
Today, I see much clearer

Look at Me Now

Marvelous

Even in my sin
Your blood
You shed

Who am I?
That you love me so
Though I'm grateful
I may never know

Oh how I
Marvel
at your Wonder
You never put me asunder

Your undivided grace
and mercy
and love brought me through

How excellent and perfect
JESUS
That's you!

Just believe
Your one request

Though the earth was formless
You spoke
And gave us your best

The heavens and skies
Father we say Yes

That's our humble reply

To serve you
Is my purpose
And the desire of my heart

How I Marvel
Just because you are
The day you were born
You left us a sign---A five-point star

How Marvelous you are!

It is God's Will

He wills me to life
Morning by morning
Breathing into my nostrils
It is God's Will

Smiles
And laughter
Nights and days
God's goodness
Oh how I'm amazed

It is God's Will

His Mercy and His Grace
His Words and His Presence
Moves me to stand
As I put the battle in His hands

He leads me and guides me
Beside quiet streams
For it is His will
For I am His dream

Father May your Will be done
As I hear from your Son

My Ending is Better....
Than My Beginning

Out from under the Lion's Den
Protected
Covered
Determined to win

An amazing journey
A garland of victory and beauty
My end is the beginning
My now is greater than my yesterday

Prayed and waited
Waited and listened
Listened and discovered

My New reality
That I am FREE
God did it all
For a Woman like Me...

Testimony

I'm here!

That's my testimony

Dem streets got cold
And lonely

Abuse
Misuse
Profuse neglect
But I'm here

That's my testimony

Almost lost my life
A little baby I was
But thirty three years later

I'm here

That's my testimony

Could have been dead
All of those times
I lost my head

Could have lost my mind
Battling drugs and rape
During that time

Sickness and disease
Could have claimed my flesh

God saved me
In all of my mess

He gave me His best
In the midst of the test

That's my testimony

He never left my side
Even when I wanted to hide
His love hugged me on the inside
Extinguishing my heart of pride
He sent me a woman
A messenger to bless me
In 2010, He introduced me to Tea

He told her about me before she saw my face
My presence captured her
At that moment
His desire, she embraced

That's the girl
The one you bought the bible for
This is her time
This is her gift
This is her moment

That's the truth about my testimony

Amen

As a teen
In between
Bible pages
Turning

Pew after pew
Church folks singing
Tambourines clinging
I didn't understand it
But Amen

Each time I visited
I felt a chill
Those were the times
I knew Jesus was real
I didn't understand it
But Amen!

Because I was cursed
My purpose on earth
Would not give birth

But God blessed me
Inspired me to believe
He sent a message through
a lady named Tea
I didn't fully understand
But my life was in His hands
Amen

Delivered from the grips of violence
Struggling to find inner silence

But still

I didn't understand
But Amen

My presence illuminated the atmosphere
Transcended the norm
Exposed my needs
That's when God spoke
Identifying Me!

When I was emptied out
To nothing
Tea recognized
The God in Me
She saw something

Amen and Amen again
When you are in trouble
God will send you a friend

THE BEGINNING